D1793107

APR - 1 2010	
MAR 2 6 2013	
DEC 1 8 2015	

Fritter the wasteful beastie : a beastie
 book about conserving resources /

Berry, Ron.
1993    00086836

Fritter
the Wasteful Beastie

A Beastie Book About Conserving Resources

Fritter
the
Wasteful Beastie

A Beastie Book About Conserving Resources

Written By
Ron Berry
Bartholomew
Patricia and Frederick McKissack

Illustrated By
Bartholomew

Consultants:　　Stephen W. Garber, Ph.D.
　　　　　　　　Marianne Daniels Garber, Ph.D.
　　　　　　　　Robyn Freedman Spizman

Managing Editor:　Doug Boggs
Layout Design:　　Steve Sheldon
Typography:　　　 Borst Designs
Cover Design:　　 Paul Lewis
Coloring Artists:　Donna Baker
　　　　　　　　　Gary Currant

ISBN 1-883761-02-6

Copyright © 1993 by Edu/Tainment Inc. All rights reserved. Published by Family Life Productions. No part of this book may be reproduced, copied or utilized in any form or manner without written permission from the Publisher. For information, write to Family Life Productions, P.O. Box 2710, Fallbrook, CA 92088.

Fritter is a wasteful Beastie.

She always uses more than she needs...

...And she never saves anything. Ever!

Fritter doesn't care about recycling either, so she never recycles her cans or plastics or papers.

"It's too much bother," she says. What could Fritter do to help recycle?

When Fritter takes a bath in the morning, she uses much more water than she needs.

Even when she brushes her teeth, she leaves the water running.

Fritter uses too much toothpaste, too many towels, too much toilet paper and she drys her hair for a

long, long time. What could Fritter do to not be so wasteful?

She never remembers to turn anything off when she leaves a room.

All day and all night, every light is on in Fritter's house... even when she is not at home. What could Fritter do to conserve electricity?

Fritter has a big old car that uses lots of gas. It pollutes the air with black smoke wherever she goes.

Fritter drives everywhere by herself...even to see her neighbor down the street. What could Fritter do to save gas and improve the air?

15

Fritter wastes her money too. She went to the Beastie Mall to buy her friend a birthday present.

But while at the mall, she spent all of her money playing video games. Now there is no money left to buy a birthday present.

Fritter has friends over for a special Beastie lunch. She makes lots of jelly and pickle sandwiches, gizzard gumbo, lizard pie and rutabaga cookies. Mmmmm…Good!

Oh, no! Fritter has made too much food! "Don't worry," she says.

"What we don't eat we'll throw away." What should Fritter do instead?

When Fritter does her homework and makes one small mistake, she crumples up her paper and starts all over again.

She never thinks to use an eraser.

Fritter likes her house cold in the summer. So she turns the air conditioner on high. Brrrrrrrrr.

In the winter, she doesn't like to wear a sweater or use a blanket, so Fritter sets the heater on high. How could Fritter help to conserve energy?

It doesn't bother Fritter that she wastes, and wastes, and wastes.

She always says, "Who cares, there's plenty more." What would you like to tell Fritter?

Fritter is a wasteful Beastie.

She never conserves anything. What about you?

A person who is wasteful has no regard for the valuable resources in our world.

If you want to be a good citizen of Planet Earth, you can do these things:

Food
Don't waste food by taking more than you can eat. And eat whatever you take.

Water

When you take a bath or shower, don't use more water than you need. Turn off dripping water faucets.

Energy
Turn off appliances and lights in rooms that are not being used.

When going someplace, walk or ride a bike if possible. Don't ask to be driven unless it is necessary.

Ecology

Don't be a litterbug. Put your trash in a trash can. Help your family recycle plastics, cans, glass and newspapers.

Money
Use your money wisely. Don't waste it by buying things that you will not use.

E BER
Fritter the wasteful beastie : a beastie
 book about conserving resources /
Berry, Ron.
1993   00086836